MW01290005

In this collection C.J. Prince offers an unflinching look at childhood with the mother and child seeking balance. That certain tension between generations is illuminated head-on. Incredibly tender moments in a woman's life are revealed. Most poignant is "Dog Days" where the child is now a mom and utterly alone while staying fully present for her children. One favorite is "Planting Scarlet Runners" where images of hands show ways for knowing family. The language is rich and clean, with some words calling up time and place so vividly I was transported back into my own life, looking at my bones in the shoe store x-ray machine. Writing with honesty and tenderness, grace and courage.

> Carla Shafer, author of *Remembering the Path*
> Bellingham, Washington

A brilliant, intricately woven rendition of stigmas, family rules, love and pain that stains the soul.
A highly recommended read.

> Una Bruhns, poet, creative writer
> Vancouver, BC, Canada

C.J. Prince's poems brim with tenderness, compassion and empathy. In this autobiographical collection abounding in images from BB guns to drowned kittens, the shadow cast by her mother, "born too early for the age of Aquarius," inhabits the pages either as a bodily presence, a memory, or as a ghost who is "not here" but "everywhere," and whose "words rise up like dandelions in spring." These poems, at times both funny and sad, ask the unanswerable questions, deal with "the ways of love" as well as "the weft of pain," and reveal to discerning readers that forgiving can indeed be a two-way street.

> Paul Fisher, author of *Rumors of Shore,*
> Bellingham, Washington

Brilliant. A magnificent book.

C.J. Prince's poems are emotionally moving and intricately described interactions and conversations between mother and daughter covering several decades. With precise details to bring each encounter alive, this daughter maps moods between them to discover that she still honors her mother's quirky advice as a cornerstone to her own values. Talking with parents never stops.

Poet C.J. Prince writes a moving, honest tribute to her mother that vividly depicts a certain time and culture. Her poems mix love, sadness and disappointment as she recreates her childhood and her escape from it. All children are captives of a complex and contradictory world they must figure out in order to survive. C. J., like all of us, is still figuring it out, examining the pieces, putting them in their natural patterns, learning, integrating, forgiving and freeing herself. She takes us on her journey through a world of soda pop and gasoline, guns and Sunday School, of shoes, make-up and jewelry, no laughter and bad choices, kindness and cruelty. It's a work of art you won't forget.

Mother, May I?

martini
forget **don't**
olive tart
bar martinis sip
suck you're library
road wait voice publication
reach retrieval **book** **mother**
bite stored
snatch photocopying author
juice **written published**
stuart quote
friday charlotte **green**
glass 1913 reproduced eighteen
runs head
sits pimiento electronic
drink **laugh**
atop **doesn't** shiny
elbow **mother's**
jackson

Poems

By

C.J. Prince

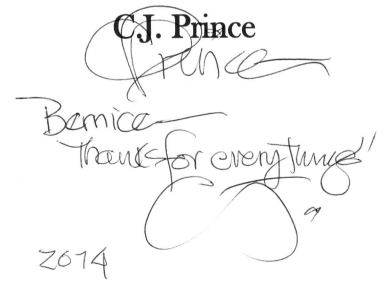

Bernice
Thanks for everything!

2014

Prince, C.J.
Mother, May I?

Copyright 2014 by C.J. Prince

ISBN-13:
978-1500510084

ISBN-10:
1500510084

Edited by
Andrew Shattuck McBride
Format Design by Joanne McLain
Cover Design by Flannon Jackson

Published by Ravens' Song Press

For Florence Charlotte Stuart Prince
aka Peachy Prince
1913-1985

Cheerleader, Carpinteria Union High School
1931

Mother, May I?

Contents

Mother, May I?

Waiting for the Red Eye

Friday nights they forget
"Don't."

Don't is the first word
I remember—a voice from above.
Don't doesn't mean anything
if you're eighteen months old.

Adults on the couch laugh,
sip martinis. I reach
for the giant green olive
with a pimiento dot
like a comic book eye.
Mother's stern look flashes
a warning that might alert father.
I wait, play with wooden blocks.

Mom pulls out a cigarette, Dad flicks a Zippo.
A blue haze circles around me. They drink
and then an empty glass is lowered.
I snatch the shiny green treasure,
suck tart juice, bite into the chilled olive.
Martini juice dribbles to my elbow.

Chug-a-lug

Saturday and Dad wears a blue work shirt,
sleeves rolled, and dungarees.
I clamber into the old '46 Chevy pickup
with three on the floor.

It's a mile down Toro Canyon,
a long mile when I walk.
A quick ride with Dad
to the Richfield station

where I breathe deeply
enjoying the rich aroma
of gasoline,
but it is the icy cold bottle

of Delaware Punch
that flows down my throat—
  glug glug glug
easy no choking bubbles—

that I crave.
Our small refrigerator on the back porch
never stocked soda pop
or unnecessary items.

One Christmas my godmother
gave me a perfume bottle
of gasoline.
They laughed. I sniffed.

Gasoline noxious with all the additives
doesn't smell the same now
and I haven't seen a Delaware Punch
in decades.

Sunday School

She chewed on the bristly end of her pigtail
and squinted at the black and white film.
Gonna eat your hair? an older boy teased.
She dropped the red rope.

Fidgeting, she stared hard.
A man played god.
How could that be?
Make no graven image.
Not graven but an image moving.
How is that different?

She was eight.
No one gave her an answer.
Even her mother didn't know.

I Remember

After Joe Brainard

I remember a gallon jar no longer
holding pimiento-stuffed martini olives,
a jar jam-crammed with marbles
pushed to the back of the wardrobe
where my brother wouldn't find it.
Me, good with a steelie, shooting straight,
collecting, hiding all the boys' marbles I won.

I remember they had BB guns and shot birds—
me running down by the bridge
past the orange grove—flapping my arms,
"Fly, birdie, fly."
I remember shouldering the 4/10 rifle
as my father taught me to aim down the sight
and hit a distant tin can.
I remember my step-brother-to-be shooting frogs
in the swamp where we built a raft.
I remember bright green-yellow ooze
from a dead frog's body.

I remember a loaded gun
in the buffet at my mother-in-law's house.
I remember being a pacifist,
belonging to Another Mother for Peace,
not allowing toy guns
in my children's playroom.
I remember they shot with sticks.

I remember shoulder high jade plants
growing at the back door
where the calico cat Daisy left gopher entrails
or her latest batch of kittens my father would drown.

4

I remember my mom
driving the weapons carrier
they bought after the war,
our only transportation. She painted the frames
of her sunglasses glaring red with nail polish.
I remember the Navy ship on endless gray seas
as we sailed out of the Azores
to go ashore in Casablanca.

I remember the fear of being whipped.
I remember not wanting to take the garbage out
because possums with long harsh tails
slashed around the can
near the *Copa d'oro* twining on the garage.

I remember my mother flipping open
the wringer washer that caught my braid.
I remember my grandmother's piano
and my fingers picking out "Silent Night."

Sour and Sweet

Clamber off yellow bus,
climb the hill.
Olive trees spike
fiesta red blooms.

Snap tender stalks
of lemon grass.
Bite, suck green stems.
Face puckers.

Tromp through cool shade
of eucalyptus grove,
feet crunch layered debris.
Drag hand
across leaves in lemon orchard.

Stop to spit over bridge.
Clutch nose and sprint
past the billy goat's paddock
under the oaks.

Hug Nanna in her
faded feed-sack apron.
Sink teeth in melting
chocolate chip cookies
at gray house
under the pine.

Smelling of Chanel No. 5 and Lucky Strikes,
Mom picks me up. We drive home
after they sip a sherry.

Learning to Genuflect

She wears
a beribboned boater
atop red pigtails
and shiny, new-once-a-year
Mary Janes,
wiggles her fingers
in new white Easter gloves,
follows Mother down the aisle.

She doesn't understand
heaven or hell
but kneels upright
even when her knees hurt.

When in Rome: The Evolution of Style

You wear sturdy brown oxfords,
Buster Browns you try on at Levy's shoe store
on State Street. You ease your foot
into stiff brown leather,
slide those shoes into slots on a machine.
You lean forward, over the big brown unit,
peer down at your chartreuse skeletal feet,
wiggle your toes, laugh at bouncing bones.

In Naples you wear handmade sandals
of fine Italian leather, wear holes in the soles
as you climb Mt. Vesuvius.

In Casablanca your mother buys green sandals
that lace up to her knees,
leather cured in camel urine.
When you're in high school,
she gives them to you.

In London, you polish black oxfords
to an obsidian shine,
wear gray knee socks
below a pleated flannel skirt.
You don a gray matching blazer
with avocado green trim.
The school uniform includes a white shirt
and that special school-green tie.

In high school you wear saddle shoes,
rolled down socks
or white flats and pink crinolines
under billowing skirts.

Aging feet seek comfort. You try SAS,
so boring,
without the bounce of a Z Coil.
Naturalizers seem unnatural.
Not all tennis shoes are for playing tennis,
nor are they comfy.

You drift to orthopedic
old lady shoes,
with heavy wool socks
to accompany comfortable clothing.
Yet your feet need more.
Teva offers summer bliss
with a sculpted foot bed.
Now you need a lift for the one inch
difference in leg length.
Your latest find, Skecher Rockers,
feel good on the feet, give you balance
and your lower back doesn't scream.

Every year, every season,
you tie it all together
with jewelry:
multiple rings,
a wrist full of bracelets,
an anklet and toe rings.

Your grandfather was right.
Shoes are the most important
part of your wardrobe.

What Counts?

If Santa arrives at 5 p.m.
the night before,
and sloshes a martini or three

every Christmas,
it is only that one time he swings in
with a bottle of single malt scotch

and hands her a sourball
on the Isle of Capri
that she remembers.

It is not the rack of lamb
all trussed up like a crown,
when the family tensions

merge with mint jelly
and lemon meringue pie,
that she remembers.

But oranges plucked from the tree
and her grandmother's raw-knuckled
hand on hers,

a touch lasting a lifetime,
dependable, always there
when nothing else was.

Tar

My red hair
reeks
like Torito Road
on a hot summer day,
when tar swelled
into iridescent mounds
sticking to bare feet.
A new shampoo
to relieve itching.

I think
buckets of tar,
tar paper, roof tar,
tar on the beach.
Mother cleaned
my tar-spotted feet with gasoline.

I loved the smell
of gasoline, fresh
from the pump at the Richfield station,
now hate the acrid stench
of tar shampoo
that will heal
my scalp.

Mother said
You must suffer for beauty.

Lost Plaits

Under the kitchen table
I played pickup sticks.
When I heard my name,
I scooted closer,
peered through
polished chair rungs.
My grandmother's brow
creased.
Mother murmured and shrugged.
Now what had I done?

That day—my first time
at a beauty salon—
a stranger with sharp shears
cut my long red pigtails,
tossed them aside
in the wastebasket.
I looked in the mirror
at the dutch boy bob.
No one was smiling.
Especially me.

"It looks like someone
put a bowl on her head,"
my grandmother said.

"I don't have to braid it."
Mother sighed.

It was the first time
I knew I was ugly.

Neopolitan Finery

You always wore white gloves,
polished high heels, a tweed suit
and brimmed hat
to All Saints by the Sea.

In the garden you wore faded navy blue shorts
and that yellow tube top,
not bothering with makeup.

In Naples that year we lived
up in the Vomero,
we rode the *funicular* to the millinery shop.

A man measured your head,
whipped the tape from forehead to nape
and ear to ear—speaking in rapid Italian.
You spoke English.

You pointed and mimicked to show him the design
you wanted and when we returned,
the mirror captured
the elegant hat he placed on your head.
The chartreuse brim shadowed your blue eyes.

In the same shop, you placed your
elbow on the glass counter, fingers skyward.
A woman measured each digit,
ran a tape measure along the breadth
of your freckled knuckles—and then mine.

On cold Italian mornings when snow
could not damper wisps of steam
rising from Mt. Vesuvius,
we wore leather gloves like second skins.

When Mom Went to Work

Inside Fleishmann's Mansion
is a trophy room.
I stand next to
an elephant foot
half my height.

I cannot fathom
that the heads on the walls
are animals
that once roamed Africa.

Gramps, the caretaker,
goes off to check the water meter,
and monitor the thermostat.
I stand alone, small
by the elephant foot
wastebasket.

Lion, impala, springbok and warthog,
kudu, gemsbok, and blesbok;
names I cannot say,
animals I will never see alive.
Horns twisting, once flashing eyes,
dead now.
Tiger, rhinoceros, buffalo and crocodile
crowd the walls in the darkened room.

Hulking furniture
bulges beneath dusty sheets.
Glassy eyes stare from above.
I cower.

Gramps comes back.
He locks up and
we drive home.
After Grimm's bedtime stories,
I have nightmares.

Learning to Be a Girl

I remember when I was three,
we hiked in the woods.
Father followed you past poison oak and sycamores.
I rode on his shoulders as we ducked
under live oaks and I swiped
at clingy cobwebs that grabbed my face
and made nightmares.

I was afraid in the dense fog,
when we lived near the beach
and couldn't hear a warning rumble.
You took my hand, said it was safe.
Every morning we crossed the railroad tracks
when you walked me to kindergarten.

I remember we all moved into the one car garage
you and dad built. I had to clean my plate.
I hated milk sodden Wheaties.
Sometimes I missed the school bus.
You grew vegetables: zucchini and carrots,
scarlet runners, lettuce—and zinnias.
In the post war years
you planted hundreds of geraniums.

I remember you insisted
I follow Emily Post,
mind my manners,
humble myself in church
by wearing a hat.
You gave me a white rabbit fur muff
to wear to Sunday school
on foggy California mornings.
I poured martinis
at your parties when I was ten.

You let me use your *Pretty in Pink*
nail polish. Taught me how to tend my cuticles
and shape my nails.
You were there when I started my period.

That day you took me to the brassiere store
on upper State Street, I was so nervous
my stomach clenched.
A gray-haired woman slipped the small-cupped
contraption over my shoulders, told me to lean over,
so it would fit properly. You stayed outside, waiting
while I grappled with hooks and eyes
and the loss of childhood.
I was no longer a tomboy.

In high school, I hid jeans
under a full skirt with crinolines
as I left the house, drove off
in the old Chevy pickup,
then tossed my frills behind the front seat
at the end of the canyon and wore jeans to town.
You both were asleep when I came home
and shoved my skirt in the laundry basket.

"You're driving me Camarillo," you screamed
when I was a teenager, threatening
the mental hospital a few hours south.
I don't remember my transgressions.
I learned to make you a gin gimlet or Pink Lady.

El Paseo

I longed for pierced ears,
my dream since second grade
when I saw Jennie's pierced ears
threaded with red string loops.
Few people had pierced ears
in the early 50's.

Like a carrot seed waiting to sprout,
I waited for the dream.
In eighth grade it happened.
I remember that day Mom
drove us to the doctor's office
near the giant Australian bay fig tree
on lower State Street.

The small room with that medicinal smell
made me cough.
A wide window
faced down toward the harbor.
Mom thought I was scared,
said she'd go first.

First the novocaine,
her ears, then mine.
A cork, a needle.
Now, my turn. I was already light-headed
from the numbing injection.

Our ears took forever to heal
with gold starter earrings.
Then Mom took me shopping
in Santa Barbara.

We'd stepped out of the sunshine
on State Street
into the arched shadows
of El Paseo, with its unique gift shops,
galleries and restaurants
all in classic Spanish courtyards.

We squeezed into the antique jewelry store
between display cases.
I don't remember Mom's favorites.
I chose a pair of blue sapphire earrings
with a screw back—
I have only one now.

Mom wore fine jewels, pearls,
garnets, aquamarine and diamonds,
all set in gold.
I like silver and long dangly earrings.
Today I'm looking for Mom's earrings,
the pearl and jade ones,
to wear to a poetry reading.

¡Bienvenidos, Amigos!

Green satin reflects sunlight
on the Singer sewing machine
next to the bird cage,
where Winston Churchill sings
as brightly as his canary feathers.

Grandmother's age-spotted hands
cut and pin ribbons of rose red,
carnation-pink and lemon yellow,
stitching a border
around the ankle length skirt.

At thirteen, the former tomboy,
now a flower girl, walks
up State Street for Santa Barbara's
30th Fiesta Parade—her first—
a basket of summer blossoms hooked
over her elbow.

She strolls beside floats of flowers
with Spanish dancers,
mariachi bands and dancing horses.
Red curls sweep her shoulders
as she calls out one well-practiced phrase,
tossing a rainbow of blooms
to throngs of people
crowding the sidewalks:
¡Bienvenidos, amigos!

She laughs, waves at children,
rearranges the orange hibiscus
pinned behind her ear,
the white scoop-neck peasant blouse
tucked into her flowing green skirt.
Silver hoops hang from newly-pierced ears.

Later she meets the famous movie star
Leo Carrillo, wearing sterling chaps and vest,
heavy as the silver adorning his horse.

At tea time she tells her grandmother
she gave away all the flowers
before the parade ended.
But she continued to wave and call out
the new Spanish phrase to replace
more familiar playground curse words.
¡Bienvenidos, amigos!

On a Balcony Overlooking Mt. Vesuvius

He squints, checks
the archaeology of her face.
She turns her head
into the shadow
of a blue striped umbrella,
sips her martini.
He reaches for her jeweled hand.

The medical student, the married foreigner,
both know
this future can't happen.

What's the difference
between a soul and a ghost?

How Fast Do You Go?

Girls look like boys.
Guys look like chicks.
Flashfire phoenix:
Check it out.

Who do you date?
Who are you?
Who do you choose?
Who cares?

Mom says,
> *Whoever, use a condom.*

What?

> *Get an AIDS test.*

Space is fifty miles from the earth's surface.
How fast do you go?

Mother, May I?

At nine a.m.
Mom, can we go to the beach?
> *Later.*
> *When the fog burns off.*

I walk the beach in gray mist.
The shore, horizon, sky
melt together
like a chalk smudged slate.
I am invisible.
> *Don't go beyond the point.*
Seapods pop under my bare feet.

We move to Naples, Italy, a big city
where people speak words I don't know.
Mom, can I go up to the Vomero?
I've never gone alone.
> *Not alone.*
Mom!
> *Okay. Be back*
> *in half an hour.*

I walk up narrow, twisting cobbled streets,
a path I know by heart, then count endless stairs,
one step, two step, old, worn steps…
89 steps here, around the corner
more steps, 103 there…

At the top, near the *funicular*
is the rainbow man, a street vendor
with buckets of flowers.
I pick out an armload,
barter for the price
in pidgin Italian:

Voglio fiori per mia madre.
Troppo.
Take the big bouquet home to Mom.

Mom, why do I have to wear a bra?
I'm a tomboy. The boys will notice.
                    It's time.
                    Your nipples are showing.
I look in the mirror
at peanut breasts.
Really?
She doesn't hear me.
Mom, may I wear nail polish?
I look at her sunshine red nails.
                    Of course. But we'll have to see
                    what your father says.
He'll say no.
                    Just go ahead and wear it.
                    You can borrow mine.

                    Here's your own mascara.

She hands me a tiny container marked *Maybelline,*
a plastic box, red with a pullout tray.
A miniature brush rests next to the black cake.

                    Dip your brush in water like this.
                    Rub the brush, get it goopy
                    and then apply.

She leans into the mirror,
opens her mouth as she concentrates,
brushes mascara
until her pale lashes flutter black.
I do the same, jab my eye,
miss and smear my cheek

and start over.
Later father sees,
makes me scrub my face.

Mom, come here, I shout
from the toilet.
She opens the door,
                    What?
I whisper.
I think I started my period.

When the handsome man came to the door,
and met Mom, he charmed her.
Mom, can I go out with him?

                    Your father will say no, he's too old.

Mom, please.

                    She shrugs.

Neither of us know
he will take my virginity.

Note to My Dermatologist

Slathered in baby oil and iodine,
we freshman girls lounge
down at the lake
on a spring afternoon,
stretch our winter white bodies

on Missouri green grass.
Me with trembling freckles
as the others recline in aluminum
cardboard cubicles.

We adore the sun that scorches me.
When I write home to Mother,
I don't mention my flaming skin.

Two for the Road

Mrs. Jackson sits on a bar stool
stares into the mirror
behind the liquor bottles,
at her hair in a tight bun,
doesn't crack a smile.

Her hand fidgets
with an empty glass.
She nods for a second
gimlet, heavy on the Rose's.

The redhead next to her
flirts with the bartender,
laughs as he delivers
another double martini, dry.
On the house.

At 2:16 a.m.
the under-aged Mrs. Jackson
drives her redheaded mother
home and helps her into bed.
College classes in the morning,
she's glad her homework is done.
Tomorrow she needs to find
her own place.

Mama

I never called you *Mama*.
I'm sitting in a sunbeam
that slipped through a cloud today.

You wouldn't like the long rainy winter here.
You liked it hot with fried freckles
and a morning Schlitz.

You never came to visit me
after I left.
Did I forget to invite you?

Or was it your horrid boyfriend?
Was he missing one or two legs?
He tried to kill my cat.

Did I forget to invite you?
I didn't have a phone.
I wrote, didn't I?

I loved you, you know?
Even if you had bad taste
in men.

You deserved better
but didn't know it.
I loved you

even then
when I never wanted
to see you again.

Affirmation for Women of a Certain Age

I will not be that little old lady
    with hair on my chin,
      says the little old lady with hair on her chin.

I will not be a porcupine chin
    she mutters and pats a hand for misplaced glasses,
    peers into magnifying mirror,
    fingers search for hair spikes.

I will not offer kisses that rake young cheeks,
    she says, remembering great aunts
    with bad breath and whiskered chins.

I will not…
    and for a moment,
    she can't recall what she will not.
    In her morning shower
    while shaving her legs,
    she remembers her prickly pear chin,
    swipes the razor at offending chin sprouts,
    knicks flesh. Bright blood runs.

Perhaps I will be a little old lady with a bristly chin.

It Takes as Long as It Takes

Adeline clutches the rock heavy iron box
of crushed bones, crumpled debris,
all that's left of Wally.

She comes for tea,
lowers Wally onto the Victorian chair beside her.
    I haven't changed the sheets, she says,
    I still wear his T-shirts, pauses,
    for the smell of him.
She looks out the window toward grazing sheep.

Local gossips call her crazy.
    She should scatter the ashes,
        they say to each other.
The family complains.
        Scatter the goddamn ashes.

Wally goes everywhere with her:
to the A & W, to the library, to Safeway,
on walks where she feeds stray dogs.

Three years after Wally's death,
She walks along County Road 98 at dusk.
Wally's ashes fly above yucca,
settle on Ponderosa needles,
fill the plains with light.

Dog Days

The angle of late morning sunlight
cracks Indian summer hot, desert air
on brittle roadside weeds.

A piercing yelp.
I turn, look,
run barefoot,
feet flying over crisp brown grass,
toe-stubbing pebbles,
my children, five and seven, at my heels.

I do not remember blue and pink flowers
on my hand sewn skirt, my only skirt.
I gather, cradle the whimpering pup.
Do my children cry?   Do I?

Neighbors who won't speak to hippies
gather to watch.
The driver hauls himself out of his car,
hands on hips,
mouth full of angry words.

"Please," I cry.
"I have no car."
"Please," I beg.
"Take us to the vet."

"No. It's too late," the voice, gruff.
My body quivers, my hands shake,
heart pounds a wild rhythm.

"Pumpernickel—"
the name my son gave his pup—
I say, *"it's okay,"*
over and over,
"It's okay,"
and stroke the golden brown fur.

The driver gets in his car. Gravel spews,
tires burn rubber pattern to pavement.
Gawkers fade back behind locked doors.
"Please…"
But it is too late.

We sit at the roadside in hot sun,
gravel bruises flesh
until the pup's body is cold.
Dried streaks of salt
seersucker cheeks.

If We Could Talk

I don't remember your laughter.
At day's end, makeup faded,
Alluring Red crawled up your lip line.
You stirred the aluminum dinner pot.

I don't remember your hug.
When I sliced my thumb on a sharp knife
washing dishes the water turned pink.
You gave me two weeks off.
My brother grumbled at full-time duty.

I could call you "Mom."
Not like father who insisted on "Sir."
You didn't laugh.

I remember the sex talk.
Matter of fact and without shame.
By then your husband wandered
away for his pleasures.

"You have to suffer for beauty,"
you said and showed
me how to curl
my eyelashes.
"Sir" made me scrub my face.

You worked two jobs, I remember.
On weekends, you'd sit in a captain's chair
on the patio, smoke Camels, drink
Old Milwaukee and nibble Hershey bars.
You didn't laugh.

You let me keep the cat who peered
in the open door
that year I had the mumps.
It cheered me. There was a row.
"Sir" yelled and hollered.
I kept the cat that had two litters
every year until she died.

You let me read your books.
Some of the grown-up ones
I couldn't give a book report on.
It was our secret.

Did you laugh with your mother?
Or was that the only place to shed tears?

I don't remember your laughter—
unless you'd had three double martinis.

Planting Scarlet Runners

Young hands tighten
violin strings.
Her chin tucks, eyes close,
bow slices.

Strong hands warp
a loom and weave
the green and white table runner
for the fireplace mantle.

Tired hands push
soggy clothes
through the wringer washer.

Days-end hands select a Chesterfield
from the yellow cloisonné
cigarette case,
flick a Zippo and relax.

Impatient hands that braid
my red hair,
plant scarlet runners,
knit a beige suit
of knobby yarn.

Freckled hands grasp
a silver martini shaker
and pour a dry one.

Kind hands drape
a heated cloth mustard plaster
on my chest.

On Saturday morning she tosses
a shot of Jim Beam with one hand,
followed with an Old Milwaukee chaser.

White gloved hands
fold in prayer
as she kneels on Sunday mornings,
then walks to the altar
for communion.

Weekday hands
scrubbed clean for work,
fingernails painted *Fire and Ice*
with gold rings sparkling.

Hands that flip
pages of *The New Yorker*,
gather library books,
receive the latest from
Book of the Month Club.

Tear spattered hands
chop onions, jalapeños
and tomatoes to make chili sauce
for neighbors at Christmas.

Weary hands fold clothes,
scrub the toilet,
polish sterling silver,
keep a journal,
hide liquor bottles
in old purses.

Hands that tally
figures for a Chinese restaurant
at night,
her second job.

After her husband's abuse,
scented hands
that once stroked
a young Italian lover.

Cold still hands.
Shroud bound now.

Inside Out

Please forgive me
if I don't smile,

if I don't let you into the wound
that is not yours,

shards of failures
and limping doubts that limp on crutches.

If I let you see behind my joy,
you might drown in tears unshed.

You might tumble
into the labyrinth of pain.

What if you hate
my shadow side?

Were you to see the cracks, the dents,
the ruts that sink deep,

you would find a bit of my soul.
If I don't smile,

The Milky Way will not dissolve.

Hair

Summer bears down
like dragon's breath
as I drive the battered '62 Volvo,
an overgrown VW bug,
heater stuck on high in every season.

My red hair falls below the waist,
rests like a shoulder blanket.
I snatch it back into a manageable rope,
the same hair I unwind
and place on my children's wounds,
every cut and scrape tended
with my magic hair,
no band-aids required.

After sleepless nights
twisted in hot, rumpled sheets,
long hair sticking to sweaty body,
after days of silent deliberation,
I make the decision
to cut it. Cut all my hair off.

I stop the woman who walks past my house,
a stranger with a do called a shag.
She recommends her salon
in far-off Hollywood.

LA summer heat sizzles.
Windows down as I suck
the last dregs of a roach,
exit Hollywood Boulevard.

A few strands of red hair escape
the single rope of red braid.
I swipe them aside,
wipe sweat from my brow
with the back of my hand.

The salon, upscale, hot, hip, air conditioned.
Bright lights, fast talk, the Rolling Stones
loud on big speakers.
You Can't Always Get What You Want.
My thighs stick to the faux leather seat.
For a moment, I hate my miniskirt.

The stylist in four-inch heels, leggings
and a loose tie-dye number evaluates me,
her sleek black hair swept back.
Aloof eyes catch mine in the mirror.
She grabs my braid, reaches for shears
and changes her mind to find larger,
sharper ones.
A crushing *crunch*—it begins—
the sound of metal
forced through fiber
as she clips my hair,
a sensation that echoes
for days. I am light-headed.

A battalion of hair dryers,
shiny chrome domes of roaring heat.
People everywhere in all stages
of beauty madness.
Thioglycolic acid fumes race to my nostrils.
A bevy of handsome young men
who only wash hair.

I stare at the blunt ends of a bowl cut,
second grade fear rising up.
I will not cry.
Mother and Father both had red hair.
Mom would like this place.

Clip snip clip clip clip—
The stylist begins shaping.
I watch in the mirror and see
my braid—alone and long—
now captured by a heavy green
rubber band, abandoned on the counter.
She pauses. I reach out,
clutch the braid with grieving hands.
I'll give it to him. He'll understand.
I never told him.
I told no one. Not a soul who would
interfere, who would say, *No, don't do that.*
I just came here, silent,
with secretive Scorpio rising.
Now I must tell him.

When I tell him, I will hand the red rope to him.
He is four. It will be his now.

The hair I unwind and place
on his wounds, his cuts and scrapes,
the healing hair.
Detached, I fear it is meaningless.

Fact or Fancy?

There's no dealing with you.
The lake trail is one point two miles.
Your secrets are covered in sugar.
The population of Bellingham is 81,862.
Your truth lies in an FBI file.
There are rocks in the clouds.
Will you forgive me?

Too Early for the Age of Aquarius

If you were born in 1913,
if you thought those rules
would always apply,

if you cried on your wedding day
and stopped playing
the violin forever,

because your groom didn't like it,
if you canned peaches, beans
and tomatoes to save money,

if you worked
when other women didn't,
grew vegetables, sipped Hamm's and tossed shots,

and folded towels your own way,
and read endless books,
you could remember being the life of the party.

If you didn't finish college
because there was a war
and you went to work,

and somehow what you thought was love
was less,
you found your own way.

If no one went to a therapist,
no one had ADHD,
or no one cared

if you had an extra martini
so you wouldn't see
your best friend having sex

with your husband.
You had another drink,
and felt pain in your left arm.

If you were born in 1913,
you never heard of assertiveness training,
never knew the comfort of a women's group,

only the idle promise of a well-soaked
martini olive
as you worked those years
while others played canasta.

You would knit a flowing skirt
of knubby yarn on fine needles
but could not knit your life together.

You did the only thing you knew.
You ordered a double martini for work lunch.
Home on weekends, you made an avocado sandwich

on soggy white bread with mayonnaise,
drank a brew
and curled under the brown and gold afghan,

to sleep away your weekends
avoiding your Capricorn daughter
as she embraced the sixties.

You were born too soon,
Aquarian woman.

How To Sleep

When I suck my thumb,
Mother red peppers it
like a lamb chop.

Just go back to sleep,
Mother says when I crawl into her bed.
Don't put your hands between your legs.

Once I taste liqueur in Mother's crystal decanter
but squinch my face.
Sometimes I hide under the covers
and read by flashlight.

Warm milk, my grandmother's solution.
Coffea, a homeopathic remedy, doesn't work either.

Later pale blue Valium makes me sleepy all day.
Tryptophan works until it's pulled off the market.
Try three milligrams of Melatonin, the doctor says.

With five milligrams of generic Ambien,
the dream wolf
guides me to the gates of darkness.

Acupuncture drops me into the center
of silence, meridians flow
like the flight of a pollen-laden bee.

After You Left

I planted sweet roses along the trellis.
Overgrown, they hang heavy with bees.
I sought but am not sought, staring
beyond honeysuckle and Black Mary.
I am lost as night birds sing,
on my knees.

Your Grave Is Overgrown

No
time to say hello.
My umbrella flips
inside out, metal spikes
like a rowdy robot head.
Wind blusters
my tidy hair sideways.

No time to check a mirror.
No time to answer my cell,
to see the deer,
to send a text.
No time to cook from scratch,
to do a load of laundry.

No time to buy cat food.
No time to hug.
A tree calls me,
wet and dark,
waiting, cedar arms open.
No. I can't say
No to a ring of cedars.

Yes, I will stop the clock
and scrub your marble
on All Saints' Day—

trim back the crabgrass,
and tend your parent's graves
at your side.

A Valediction Forbidding Mourning
After John Donne

The Family Rule Book sits scarred and tattered,
center stage on the polished mahogany buffet,
where bone china dishes of great aunts
hide on faded green felt separators,

where sterling silver knives and forks
wait for the next command performance.
The Family Rule Book
guides generations.

On page 91, just below the sherry stain,
is where the Rules on Dying begin.
First, do not. Do not do it in public.
Do not let others know you will do it.

Deny all outer signs of decay.
Do not talk of others doing it.
Never mention a will.
Do not consider cremation, crypt or tomb.

When others do it, do not cry.
Mind your manners.
Carry a silk hankie, wear black.
Feign remorse.

Wear false eyelashes to funerals.
Vanity will forestall tears.

Where Are You?

Mother's bristled chin
droops to her chest.

The hospital gown sags askew
across her once pearl-adorned neck,
now veined and boney.
Her throat is empty of words.

Opaque-blue eyes stare through me.
Almost a decade of not knowing
anyone. Not knowing me.

"How are you, Mom?"
Iodine, she mutters.
I lean forward.

Does she have a cut
or did she just dine?

We sit facing each other,
our knees nearly touching,
save for the wheelchair footrests.

"Hi, Mom." I try again.
She does not answer.

A worn strap—waist to shoulder—
holds her frail body
upright.

Her eyes brighten,
rivet on my mirror blue ones.
What do you want me to do?

The first clarity in eight years—
just like the psychic told me long ago:
Your mother will recognize you,
know you before she dies.

"Whatever you want, Mom."
My thumb moves over
the valleys and mountains
of her knuckles.

"You don't have to stay here.
It's okay to go.
I'll be okay.
It's your choice," I say.

Her eyes unlatch
from mine, gone now
to that separate reality.

Five weeks
and three days
later,
she leaves
her body shell.

What Does She See?

Mother's words rise up
like dandelions in spring.

Hack, whack or mow them down
and still they rise again.
You must suffer for beauty.

I wonder now
if she or I can even define
the details or the results.

I see the little lines of life
become creases
and then crevices.

Mirror, mirror are you true?
What does suffering require?
A little gold chain

edging from ear to ear
tucked under,
to hold up a double chin?

Or a surgeon's scalpel
to make my face a drum
so tight I cannot smile?

I wonder
if that's what Mother meant.
What was her other expression?

Beauty is only skin deep.

Hear Me Beyond the Grave

Mother,
Mother Mary,
Great Mother Goddess,
My Mother,
Mother Peachy,
come to me.

Forgive me.
Forgive my sins,
the errors of my youth.

Mother Peachy,
come to me with comfort,
whisper sweet in your soul voice.

Forgive me my willfulness.
Forgive me my ignorance.
Forgive my sins.

I forgive you.

Ocean Breezes Blow on Black Marble

Your lemon-scented soul touches me,
a wisp of essence gliding along foothills,
seeping into canyons of memory
alive with oak and *ceanothus*.

My bare toes inch closer to the black marble
etched with your name, your dates—
contradictions of life and death battle for balance.

You no longer weep
beneath sycamores. The violin is silent,
the martini glass empty. Your geraniums
still bloom in my garden.

The warp of love, the weft of pain
dissolve into the veil.

You are not here.
You are everywhere.

ACKNOWLEDGEMENTS

Thanks to WOW, Write on Women, my writing critique group, to whom I am ever grateful: Carol Austin, Nancy Canyon, Harley Crowley, Shannon Hager, Susan J. Erickson, and Rae Ellen Lee for patience and wisdom in editing my poetry.

Thanks to the Muse-icians, my weekly writing practice group for keeping me honest, fresh and in the moment: Anny Edmonds, Barbara Gobus, Linda Hirsh and Pam Weil. Thanks to First Friday Writers for diving deep and bubbling with laughter.

Thanks to all the open mics for the opportunity to read and refine my poems. Gratitude all the way back to my high school English teacher, Marjorie Holmes, and forward to all who continue to encourage me. If I know you, you are part of my process, have influenced my insights and for that I am grateful.

Deep appreciation to Andrew Shattuck McBride for his insights and precision in editing. Thanks to Joanne McLain for continued support and all her technical skills in formatting *Mother, May I?* to book form.

Gratitude and thank you are not enough for Michael E. Berg, my partner who endures and copes with my piles of notes, stacks of re-writes, boxes of manuscripts and mid-sentence pauses to write down a word or idea or brilliant phrase when I am under the spell of the Muse.

C.J. Prince

C.J. PRINCE

Novels

The Fondis Chronicles
  With Joanne McLain and William C. Thomas

Catching My Breath
  With Joanne McLain and William C. Thomas

Chapbook

Twenty Four Houses

"Chug-a-lug" was previously printed in the
Carpinteria Historical Society publication.

"It Takes as Long as It Takes" was previously
published in the *2013 Whatcom Writes!* anthology.

Colophon

Mother, May I?, published in July 2014, is C.J. Prince's second collection of poetry. This edition is printed in 11 point Garamond font. Formatting and layout by Joanne McLain, Parker, Colorado. Cover art by Flannon Jackson, Brooklyn, NY.

Made in the USA
San Bernardino, CA
31 August 2014